A Medical Provider's Survival Guide to Injury Claims in Misso



# MAXIMIZING REIMBURSEMENT FOR INJURY PATIENTS

K|J|M

LAW OFFICE OF

KEVIN J. MCMANUS

**Kevin J. McManus**
**Law Office of Kevin J. McManus**
**1100 Main Street, Suite 2600**
**Kansas City, MO 64105**
**www.KevinMcManusLaw.com**
**Phone: 816-203-0143**


**1st Edition**



**Printed in the United States of America.**

**ISBN: 978-0-692-13834-2**

**$16.95**

***Have you ever failed to receive payment for a patient who was injured in a car accident, slip and fall, work injury or other personal injury accident?***

# Read Inside to Learn How to Maximize Medical Reimbursement for Injury Claims in Missouri and Kansas.

**Including:**

- **8 Billing Myths for Medical Providers**
- **7 Common Billing Mistakes Made by Medical Providers**
- **What is the Best Source for Medical Reimbursement?**
- **What is the Best Billing Method for the Patient?**

<u>LEGAL DISCLAIMERS:</u>
THE INFORMATION IN THIS BOOK CONTAINS GENERAL STATEMENTS AND IS NOT INTENDED AS LEGAL ADVICE OR LEGAL OPINIONS. THIS BOOK DOES NOT CREATE AN ATTORNEY-CLIENT RELATIONSHIP. YOU SHOULD NOT ACT OR RELY UPON THE INFORMATION IN THIS BOOK WITHOUT SEEKING THE ADVICE OF AN ATTORNEY BECAUSE CHANGES IN THE LAW OCCUR FREQUENTLY AND YOU SHOULD CONSULT WITH AN ATTORNEY WITH RESPECT TO YOUR PARTICULAR SITUATION. ADVERTISING MATERIAL: THE CHOICE OF A LAWYER IS AN IMPORTANT DECISION AND SHOULD NOT BE BASED SOLELY ON ADVERTISEMENTS. PAST RESULTS AFFORD NO GUARANTEE OF FUTURE RESULTS AND EACH CASE IS DIFFERENT AND IS JUDGED ON ITS OWN MERITS.

# WHO WROTE THIS BOOK AND WHY?

Thank you for requesting this book on how to maximize medical reimbursement for injury claims in Missouri and Kansas. I hope this book gives medical providers the knowledge and tools they need to ensure prompt payment for the treatment they provide to injury patients.

For many years, I have represented individuals in Missouri and Kansas who have been injured in accidents. In my experience, the interests of our clients and their medical providers are interrelated and interdependent.

When our clients get prompt and proper treatment, they move faster on the road to recovery. Their claims are better documented and more fairly valued by adjusters. This helps them get resolved sooner with a better outcome.

All of this can be a major benefit for their medical providers who may have bills that need to be paid from settlement proceeds. I know this is true from my own experience with our clients' medical providers. They have told me they appreciate the procedures our law office uses that both benefit our clients and maximize reimbursement. Some have even asked me how they can improve their medical billing practices. After a little research, it became apparent that there was a need for helpful and detailed information on this subject. This is why I decided to write a book on how to maximize reimbursement in Missouri and Kansas injury cases.

If your office is like most, there are still times where payment is never received for a patient who was injured in a car accident, slip and fall, work injury or other personal injury accident. As detailed in this book, the proper procedure and "best practices" for billing vary depending on the type of case. This book dispels the myths and answers the most commonly asked questions about medical billing and payment for each of these types of cases.

I hope this book is helpful to you and those who provide important medical treatment for our clients. If you have questions, please feel free to call our office. We would be happy to be a resource to you on this subject or any legal issue.

Sincerely,

Kevin McManus

Kevin McManus

www.KevinMcManusLaw.com

- Attorney representing individuals injured in vehicle and other accidents
- Named "Best of the Bar" by *Kansas City Business Journal*
- Recognized by *SuperLawyers* Magazine as a "Rising Star"
- Licensed in Kansas and Missouri with active trial practices in both states
- Graduate of Roberts Trial Academy, Kansas City Metropolitan Bar Association
- Member of City Council in Kansas City, Missouri, with extensive knowledge and experience in transportation and infrastructure laws
- Former member of the Missouri House of Representatives and recipient of legislative award from the Missouri Bar for contributions to civil justice issues
- Author of numerous consumer books and reports

# 8 Medical Provider Billing Myths

1. Having an injury patient sign a "lien form" will create a legally enforceable lien and ensure you are paid.
2. You will be promptly paid if you submit your bills to the insurance company for the negligent party or at fault driver in an injury case (also known as the liability insurance company).
3. Naming the patient's attorney as the guarantor on a medical bill will guarantee the bill is paid.
4. Bills submitted to a patient's health insurance for an injury case will typically be denied.
5. It is always good idea to wait until the end of the case to obtain full payment of the bill instead of accepting an amount with a write-off.
6. If a patient has medical payments or personal injury protection coverage, you should submit all bills to that insurance company because they always pay.

7. In a workers' compensation case, you should submit the bills to the employer and/or the workers' compensation insurance company, and you will be paid.
8. Unlike car accident cases, medical payments coverage is not a source of reimbursement in slip and fall cases.

***The purpose of this book is to dispel these myths and offer practical advice on how to get paid.***

## Myth #1: Lien Forms

Some medical providers require a patient to sign a "lien form" before agreeing to treat the patient. They do this because they believe this form will guarantee payment. Unfortunately, this is not true. The injured patient's attorney is not bound by the "lien form," and insurance companies are not either. The patient can choose to ignore the form, and this will force the provider to seek reimbursement from the patient directly.

Medical provider liens are only legally enforceable if they comply with applicable state law. The Kansas hospital lien statute that details the Kansas requirements is K.S.A. § 65-406 et seq. The Missouri medical lien statute is Mo. Rev. Stat. 430.225 et seq.

In Kansas, only hospitals can assert a lien on a personal injury claim. Kansas law sets out a specific procedure and conditions that hospitals and clinics must follow before the lien is enforceable. For example, Kansas law requires the eligible lienholder to send notice of the lien. The notice must include the amount of the lien, the name of the injured person, the date of the accident and the name and location of the hospital. Kansas law requires this notice to be filed in Kansas district court where the hospital is located and sent to the injured person by certified mail.

In Missouri, a lien on a personal injury claim can be asserted by a hospital or clinic, as well as a licensed physician or surgeon, chiropractor, podiatrist, physical therapist, dentist or optometrist. Missouri law also requires an eligible lienholder to provide written notice of a lien. The notice must include the name of the injured, date of the incident, and names of those alleged to be responsible for the accident. This notice must be sent by certified mail to all parties responsible for reimbursement, which may include insurance companies, the injured person, or the person who caused the accident.

## Myth #2: Submitting Bills to Liability Insurance

Submitting your bills to the insurance company for the negligent or at-fault driver does not ensure they will be timely paid. The insurance company for the at-fault party in a car accident will wait until the case or claim is resolved before agreeing to pay any money for medical bills. This could take years.

Also, when the claim is resolved, it is unlikely that your name will be included on the settlement check or that you will be paid directly by the insurance company. For this reason, submitting bills to the liability insurance company is not a good strategy for getting paid.

## Myth #3: Patient's Attorney as Guarantor

If a client directs his or her attorney not to pay a medical provider after a claim has been resolved, then the attorney is generally required to follow the instructions of the client. As a result, putting the patient's attorney as the guarantor on the bill will not help collect the bill.

Furthermore, in some cases, this can cause real damage to the patient's case. The defense attorney and jury will see that the attorney is listed as a guarantor. The defense attorney will exploit this to his advantage and argue that the attorney must have sent the patient to the doctor and is improperly involved in the medical care.

To avoid such issues, some attorneys make their client sign an agreement that medical providers will be paid directly from the proceeds of the case. This is the practice we use at our office.

## Myth #4: Patient's Health Insurance

Your patient's health insurance company is almost always required to pay for the medical care of its insured even if the patient was injured in a car accident, work injury or other personal injury accident. The problem that sometimes arises is the insurance company denies the claim until the patient provides a form detailing to the insurance company how the injury occurred. This happens when the health insurance company also wants to be reimbursed from the settlement proceeds.

You should be aware that most health insurance companies require bills be submitted within a certain time of treatment (usually one year of the date of treatment). If that time expires, payment will be denied.

In addition, if the patient has Medicare, Centers for Medicare & Medicaid Services (CMS) has taken the position that a participating health care provider may only bill the liability insurer for its full charges during the first 120 days following accident-related treatment (also known as the "prompt pay period"). After the 120-day period, the health care provider may continue to seek payment in full from the liability insurer or may bill Medicare and accept Medicare rates as full payment.

## Myth #5: Waiting Until the End of the Case

It is usually not a good idea to wait until the end of the case to seek reimbursement from the patient. There is no guarantee the patient will receive a settlement to pay your bill. The case could get dismissed or a jury could find against the patient. This would leave you and the patient with no proceeds to distribute. Nevertheless, it is a common practice to submit bills to a patient's health insurance and to wait until the case is over to recover co-pays and deductibles from settlement proceeds.

Some attorneys will require the client sign an agreement that the medical providers will be paid directly from the proceeds of the case. This is a normal part of our injury practice and resolves this medical provider payment problem.

## Myth #6: Medical Payment or Personal Injury Protection Coverage

In certain situations, medical payment or personal injury protection coverage may be available to cover the medical bills for an injured patient. This type of insurance is also known as "no fault" insurance because it provides benefits to the injured party regardless of who caused the accident.

In Missouri, "no fault" insurance is called medical payment or "med-pay" coverage. Unlike liability or uninsured motorist coverage, Missouri drivers are **not** legally required to carry medical payment coverage. However, medical payment coverage is included in most Missouri car insurance policies.

In Kansas, "no fault" coverage is called personal injury protection or "PIP". Unlike Missouri, Kansas drivers are legally required to carry this type of insurance. Kansas drivers must have at least $4,500 per individual in PIP coverage. This minimum will cover the medical expenses of an individual injured in an accident up to $4,500.

Since med-pay and PIP coverage are paid regardless of who is at fault in an accident, insurers pay bills relatively quickly after they are submitted. For this reason, under the right circumstances, it may be best to submit the bills to the med-pay or PIP insurance company.

However, remember that there are limits on the amount of coverage available. This insurance coverage will not pay for anything above the limits. If the patient's medical bills are substantial, and the PIP or med-pay limits are low, you will need an alternative source for reimbursement.

## Myth #7: Workers' Compensation Cases

In work injury cases, the workers' compensation insurance company and/or employer has the right to choose the medical care provided to the patient. This means that, unless you are approved by the insurance company or employer, they generally will not pay your bills.

You can submit the bills to the patient's health insurance company, and in most cases, the health insurance company will pay. However, in certain rare circumstances, health insurance plans are written in such a way that if the patient seeks care outside of the approved workers' compensation doctors, it will not be paid.

## Myth #8: Slip and Fall Cases

Slip and fall cases differ from a typical car accident case in certain respects. Most obvious, a car insurance policy will not be a potential source for reimbursement. Instead, the insurance policy of the property owner, if any, is a potential source of payment.

However, the issue of comparative fault (i.e., the fault of the person who slipped and fell vs. the fault of the property owner) is fairly common in slip and fall cases. As a result, the payment through the liability provision of the insurance policy of the property owner is often disputed.

Many providers and attorneys assume that the only way to recover any amount under the property insurance policy is through negotiating or litigating the liability claim. This is not always true. Like automobile and motorcycle accident cases, there may be "no-fault" medical payments coverage in the property insurance policy. If so, this provision of the property owner's insurance policy may cover your patient's medical bills up to a certain amount regardless of who was at fault for the accident.

In most falls and other property injury claims, the amount of medical payment coverage will be relatively low, from $1,000 up to usually no more than $5,000. Also, some property owners are self-insured (businesses like Wal-Mart, Hy-Vee, etc.) and have no medical payments coverage. In these cases, the best way to maximize reimbursement is often to submit the patient's bills directly to the patient's health insurance. Nevertheless, the patient or his or her attorney should explore whether medical payment coverage exists and if it can be used to pay at least a portion of the outstanding bills quickly.

# *7 Mistakes Medical Providers Make that Prevent Maximum Reimbursement*

1. Failing to determine all possible insurance coverage available to the patient.
2. Not promptly submitting bills to the insurance company.
3. Including the incorrect dates of service on records and bills.
4. Not properly coding treatment on the records and bills.
5. Depending on the patient to pay the full amount of the bill.
6. Not clearly noting that the treatment or procedure is related to the accident.
7. Not properly preparing and filing a lien in compliance with applicable law.

## *What Can You Do to Avoid Making These Mistakes and Maximize Reimbursement?*

### 1. Identify All Applicable Insurance Coverage

The first thing to do when treating an injured patient is to determine how the injury occurred. If it appears the patient has a personal injury claim, there are likely other insurance options available beyond the patient's health insurance. For this reason, you should gather as much information from the patient regarding where the accident or injury occurred, who was involved, and whether any other party has insurance available.

If the patient was injured in an automobile accident, it is also important to identify the patient's health insurance carrier and automobile insurance carrier. There may be med-pay or PIP coverage available through the patient's car insurance that can pay a portion of the bills.

## 2. Use Proper Billing Practices

Medical bills and the processes through which they are generated can be quite complicated. This complexity only increases the likelihood of errors being made. When mistakes are made, insurance companies may refuse to pay for the patient's treatment, and providers are left with sending the bill to the patient, who may not have the ability to pay.

When insurance coverage is available, it is important to make sure bills are coded correctly. Most of the mistakes in the billing process have to do with the coding procedure. Insurance companies strictly scrutinize bills they receive. Mistakes such as entering the incorrect code, entering the wrong date of service, and/or charging the wrong rate can cause the insurance company to deny the claim.

## 3. Follow State Law Regarding Liens

As previously discussed, medical provider liens are only legally enforceable if the liens comply with applicable state law. The Missouri Medical Lien Statute (Mo. Rev. Stat. 430.225 et seq.) sets forth Missouri lien requirements, and the Kansas Hospital Lien Statute (K.S.A. § 65-406 et seq.) details Kansas lien requirements.

In Kansas, only hospitals can assert a lien on a personal injury claim. Before the lien is enforceable, Kansas law requires the eligible lienholder to send notice of the lien. The notice must include the amount of the lien, the name of the injured person, the date of the accident and the name and location of the hospital. Kansas law requires this notice to be filed in Kansas district court where the hospital or clinic is located and sent to the injured person by certified mail.

In Missouri, a lien on a personal injury claim can be asserted by a hospital or client, as well as a licensed physician or surgeon, chiropractor, podiatrist, physical therapist, dentist or optometrist. Missouri law requires an eligible lienholder to provide written notification that it intends to assert a lien. The notification must include the name of the injured, date of the incident, and names of those alleged to be responsible for the accident. Missouri law requires this notice be sent by certified mail to the parties responsible for reimbursement, which may include insurance companies, the injured person, or the person who caused the accident.

The amount of a lien is limited to the reasonable and necessary charges for the patient's treatment. If prepared properly, the provider will have a lien against any recovery collected by the patient for injuries, and the lien can be satisfied out of any settlement or judgment collected on behalf of the patient for his or her injuries.

# *How Can You Maximize Reimbursement in Car Accidents?*

Car accidents are among the most common type of personal injury accidents our law office handles. It is not uncommon for a person injured in a car, truck or motorcycle accident to incur thousands of dollars in medical treatment, even with minor accidents.

One of the best ways to ensure maximum reimbursement when treating car accident victims is to submit the bills for payment through med-pay or PIP insurance if the patient has this insurance coverage. Med-pay and PIP are types of "no-fault" insurance coverages that pay medical bills for the insured up to an amount indicated in the insurance policy.

In Kansas, drivers are required to have PIP coverage of at least $4,500 per individual for medical expenses. Kansas drivers may carry more than this minimum amount. In Missouri, med-pay coverage is not required by law, but most Missouri drivers have at least some amount of med-pay coverage in their car insurance policies. The amount of med-pay coverage can range from $1,000 to $100,000.

PIP and med-pay coverage require that medical bills must be submitted within a certain time of the accident. Generally, the time in which coverage applies ranges from 1 to 3 years from the date of a car accident.

In a car accident case, if there is significant coverage, it can be good for both the medical provider and the patient to submit bills for payment under the PIP or med-pay coverage. While the medical provider is usually paid the full amount of its bill, some insurance companies are now reviewing medical bills submitted under PIP or med-pay coverage and may reduce the reimbursements accordingly.

It sometimes can be difficult to explain to patients that it is in their best interests to submit their medical bills to their own car insurance. Patients may be concerned that their car insurance rates will go up.

They may feel that their insurance should not have to pay for medical treatment caused by someone else. You should recommend that patients talk to their insurance agent or to an attorney about this. Using PIP or med-pay coverage will not affect a patient's insurance premiums unless the patient was at fault for the accident.

There are several benefits of having medical bills paid by PIP or med-pay coverage in a car accident case, including:

- There are no co-pays or deductibles as there are when using health insurance.
- The bills are usually paid promptly instead of at the end of the case.
- The full amount of the bill is paid as long as there is enough coverage available.

If no PIP or med-pay coverage exists or the coverage has been exhausted, the next best way to ensure maximum reimbursement is to submit the bills to the patient's health care insurance.

Although it is likely the amount paid by the insurance company will be less than the amount charged, it is usually better to accept a lesser amount from the health insurer than to risk holding on to the bills and hoping the patient makes a recovery from a third party. There is no guarantee that a recovery will be made. Even if there is a recovery, it may be insufficient to cover the full amount of the bills or there may be other providers seeking reimbursement, which may make it difficult for the provider to be reimbursed fully.

## *How Do You Ensure Payment in Worker's Compensation Cases?*

To ensure payment for a patient who suffered an injury at work, you should first find out the identity of the workers' compensation insurance company and the contact information for the adjustor assigned to the case. In addition, you should ask the patient if he or she has health insurance in the event the workers' compensation insurance company does not agree to authorize you as the medical provider.

*Admitted Claim* - If it is an admitted workers' compensation claim, you may ask the insurance company to approve you as a medical care provider for the injured worker. However, it is unlikely that they will provide this approval. If they do not approve and you would still like to provide the care, you will need to submit the bills to the client's health insurance company.

*Denied Claim* - If the worker's compensation insurance company has denied the patient's claim (they may deny that it is work-related), then the patient should provide his health insurance with a copy of the denial letter, and your bills should be paid by the patient's health insurance. Providing this basic information to the patient can be very helpful in ensuring your bills are paid timely.

## *How Do You Get Paid in Other Injury Cases Like Slip & Falls, Animal Bites, etc.?*

Other types of personal injury cases include slip and falls on another person's property or animal bites. The most common slip and fall cases occur on ice or snow or tripping over objects on the ground. Like automobile and motorcycle accident cases, there may be medical payments coverage in these cases. However, this coverage is provided by the property owner as opposed to your patient.

In most falls and other property injury claims the amount of medical payments coverage will be relatively low, from $1,000 up to usually no more than $5,000. Also, some property owners are self-insured (businesses like Wal-Mart, Hy-Vee, etc.) and have no medical payments coverage.

In these cases, the best way to maximize reimbursement is often to submit the patient's bills directly to the patient's health insurance.

## *What is the Best Billing Method for the Patient?*

From a patient perspective, it is usually best to submit bills to the health insurance company first. Many health insurance plans require the patient to be responsible for co-pays, which the patient can then submit to their med-pay or PIP coverage. This billing method insures the patient will have less out of pocket expenses associated with his or her treatment.

In general, patients should look to one of the following means to seek payment of medical bills:

1. A patient's own health insurance from his or her employment benefits package.
2. A patient's own health insurance that he or she may have paid for personally.
3. Health insurance from the patient's spouse for the patient's benefit or from the patient's parents if the patient is of an age that qualifies for coverage.
4. For vehicular accidents, med-pay or PIP coverage from a patient's own insurance policy if he or she was driving when injured.
5. For vehicular accidents, med-pay or PIP coverage from the person a patient was riding with if he or she was a passenger when injured.
6. If the patient is not covered under an insurance plan they may be eligible for Medicaid.

In Kansas, KanCare is the program through which the State of Kansas administers Medicaid. The Kansas Department of Health and Environment (KDHE) and the Kansas

Department for Aging and Disability Services (KDADS) administer KanCare within the State of Kansas. If the patient is a resident of Kansas, he or she can go to a local state office or call 1-800-792-4884 for more information.

Missouri's Medicaid program is called MO HealthNet, and it is administered by the Family Support Division of the Missouri Department of Social Services. For more information about eligibility and to apply, patients can go to their local Family Support Division Office or call 855-FSD-INFO (855-373-4636).

7. The last available source for payment of medical bills is the patient's own personal funds. This is often necessary if he or she was not insured and when he or she is able to pay medical bills as they are incurred.

***Warning: Time may be running out!***

## How Long Do You Have to File a Health Insurance Claim?

Health insurance contracts impose rigid time deadlines in which to file a claim for reimbursement. These time periods vary, but usually bills should be submitted within one (1) year of the treatment date for payment. A best practice is to submit bills within thirty (30) days of treatment. The sooner you submit bills, the sooner you will know if there is going to be any issue with payment. Failure to submit bills timely may result in not being paid from insurance and instead having to collect from the patient directly, which may not be successful.

**_THE WORST THING YOU CAN DO IS DELAY OR DO NOTHING!_**

## *Does the Patient Always Need an Attorney?*

The short answer is no – some personal injury cases are small and straightforward. Car accident cases with minimum property damage, non-serious injuries, and small medical bills can often be resolved by the patient without the assistance of an attorney.

However, a patient is more likely to need an attorney in cases with more serious injuries. As the medical bills increase, it becomes critical for both the patient and the medical providers that an experienced attorney provide legal guidance and expertise so that a fair recovery can be made. An attorney is also more likely needed when the case is more complex, such as in cases involving multiple parties or if there is a dispute as to which party is liable.

# *What Are the Benefits for a Patient Hiring an Attorney?*

With more complicated or serious cases, there are many benefits to hiring an attorney. Below is a list of the actions our firm takes with most injury cases. Please keep in mind that each case is different, and not all of these actions will be required in every case.

- Initial interview with the client
- Educate our client about applicable personal injury laws and court rules
- Review and analyze the client's insurance policies to see what coverage is available to pay all or a portion of the medical bills while the claim is pending
- Gather documentary evidence, including police accident reports, medical records, films and bills

- Hire an investigator, as needed, to interview witnesses, locate witnesses, etc.
- Collect other evidence, such as photographs of the vehicles and accident scene
- Review and analyze the client's health insurance policy or other benefits plan to ascertain whether any money he or she spent to pay medical bills must be repaid
- Review and analyze all legal issues, such as comparative fault and assumption of the risk
- Provide the client a fair, unbiased opinion as to the merits of the case and the likelihood of winning
- Talk to the client's physicians or obtain written reports from them to understand the client's prognosis
- Review and analyze the validity of any liens on the case that doctors, insurance companies, welfare benefit plans and employers may assert as to the client's recovery

- Contact the insurance company to put them on notice of the claim
- Decide with the client whether an attempt will be made to negotiate the case with the insurance company or whether suit shall be filed
- If suit is filed, prepare the client, witnesses and health care providers for depositions
- Prepare and respond to written discovery, which includes requests for documents and written questions and answers from the defendant
- Prepare and take the deposition of the defendant and other witnesses
- Produce to the defendant all of the pertinent data for the claim, such as medical bills, medical records, etc.
- Conduct a scheduling conference to set a trial date
- Prepare a demand package to send to the defendant in attempt to settle the case

- Prepare for a possible mediation and/or settlement before trial
- Prepare for trial, including preparing the client and witnesses
- Organize and prepare of medical exhibits for trial
- Organize and prepare demonstrative exhibits for trial
- File motions with the court to determine what evidence will be allowed at trial
- Take the case to trial with a jury
- Review and analyze the verdict to determine if either side has good grounds to appeal the case
- Make any recommendations to the client after the verdict

## *Why Our Firm is Different*

You should know that not all attorneys approach injury cases the same way. Some attorneys practice in many different areas and may not be experienced or have the capacity to handle serious injury cases. Other firms handle hundreds, if not thousands of injury cases at a time. They may not be able to give patients and their providers the individual attention they desire.

Our firm is different. Our goal is not to be the biggest law firm in the state. We do not rely on a high volume of cases. We do not advertise on television or in the yellow pages. We do not claim to handle every kind of legal case. We do not want to do every kind of case, and frankly, we do not need to.

Our firm only accepts a limited number of serious injury and accident cases each year. We know all of our clients by their name. Unlike some "injury mill" firms, we do not accept cases with questionable merit or try to settle large numbers of cases for pennies on the dollar. Our paralegals and assistants do not negotiate cases with the insurance company. By limiting our practice and taking fewer cases, we are able to give each of our clients the attention and care that that he or she deserves, and we believe this produces better results.

We take pride in our results-driven, client-centered approach. Communication with our clients is a critical part of what we do. We explain the legal process to them, answer all their questions, and keep them informed about their case. Sometimes the best advice potential claimants may hear when they are considering a lawsuit is that they do not have a claim that can be won. If that is true, we will tell them. We will also tell them if we think that they are better off handling their claim without an attorney.

If we take a case, we share the risk with our clients because we typically advance all of the initial costs for the case. As a result, our clients will not pay any money out of pocket to get their case started. When we take a case, we fully commit to our client's cause, and we invest our time, resources and abilities to achieve the best outcome for each of our clients.

# Conclusion

I hope this book is a helpful resource for understanding the laws regarding reimbursement for injury claims in Missouri and Kansas. I know our clients are best served when our law office provides an open line of communication with our clients and their medical providers. Please do not hesitate to contact me if you have any questions or would like further information on this subject. I look forward to the opportunity to be of service to you or a mutual client/patient in the future.

# WHY EXPERIENCE MATTERS

You should be very concerned if an attorney guarantees a result based on a prior case he or she handled. Each case is different, and past results are not a guarantee of future results. Nevertheless, when selecting an attorney, find an attorney with experience in personal injury cases. A brief story illustrates why.

In late 2017, we were contacted by a couple injured in a serious car accident in Johnson County, Kansas. The husband was driving, and his wife was riding in the front passenger seat. As he entered an intersection, another car ran a red light and struck them on the passenger side in a "T-bone" collision.

The husband was not very badly injured, but his wife was seriously injured because she was sitting where the impact occurred. She had multiple broken bones and a spinal injury. Surgery was required. Medical bills grew. They sought legal guidance.

They were referred to a criminal defense attorney who supposedly did a little personal injury on the side. It is unclear what happened next, but nearly two years after the accident, they were referred to our firm. No lawsuit had been filed. No settlement offer had been made by the insurance company.

The statute of limitations for personal injury cases in Kansas is two years. This deadline is extremely important. If you do not assert all claims you have within two years, those claims are forever barred, and you will not recover a dime.

Our office pushes our cases forward so they are resolved as soon as possible. If they cannot be resolved with a pre-suit demand, we tell our client that we need to file suit, and we prepare for trial. Typically, we will not take a case if it is even close to the statute of limitations deadline.

We explained this to the couple, but they pleaded with our office to help. After reviewing the records, we discovered the reason why the insurance company was not paying them. There was no video of the crash. The husband said he had a green light, and the other driver said he had a green light. The insurance company was using their competing statements to deny paying the person who clearly was not at fault but who was most injured: the wife. She was not driving, but she was the one most badly injured. Even worse, they were saying the husband was at fault even though he was a retired professional driver with years of training and experience in safe driving.

After discussing various options and strategies with this couple, we agreed that we would represent only the wife and that we would file suit immediately against the other driver and the husband. Why? If the insurance company was going to argue that the husband was negligent, then we needed to add him as a defendant to force both insurance companies to the table. The husband and wife understood and agreed with this approach.

Within days of our filing suit and sending a demand, **BOTH** insurance companies – for the husband and the other driver – paid policy limits to our client. Each insurance company paid a six-figure amount, which in sum was well over her medical bills. Finally, the couple received fair compensation for the wife's pain and suffering.

The moral of the story is simple: experience matters. Your patient needs an attorney who has experience handling complex personal injury cases, who will investigate the facts fully and think creatively about strategies. The wrong decision can destroy a case and one's right to recover compensation for his or her injuries.

# A FEW OF OUR CASE RESULTS

Below is a sampling of cases that we have successfully resolved for clients in the past. Remember that each case is different. Once a case is in the hands of a jury, it is out of our control. However, we believe that significant trial experience in big cases is one factor that people may use to choose one attorney over another. With these things in mind, here are some of our results:

**Double Policy Limits Recovery for Passenger with Spine Injury**

Our client was a passenger who was riding with her husband when their car was struck in a "T-bone" collision. The accident occurred in Johnson County, Kansas. There was no video evidence of how the collision occurred, and the drivers had conflicting accounts. Our client's husband said he had a green light at the intersection where the crash occurred and that the other car ran a red light before colliding on the passenger side where the wife was sitting. The other driver stated she had the green light. As a result, both insurance companies – for the husband and the other driver – were disputing liability and had refused to pay. However, our client was not a fault – she was simply riding as a passenger—and she was seriously injured with multiple broken, including a broken sacrum (the large, triangular bone at the base of the spine) that required surgery. After discussing with our client, we initiated suit against both the husband and other driver, and within days, both insurance companies paid full policy limits. The settlement more than covered our client's unpaid medical bills and provided her with the compensation she deserved for her painful injuries.

## Policy Limits Settlement for Car Accident Victim Suffering Concussion

Our client was stopped at an intersection at the Country Club Plaza Shopping District in Kansas City, Missouri, when her vehicle was rear-ended by another driver. Our client's head hit the steering wheel of her vehicle on impact. She drove her vehicle from the scene to the emergency room after noticing symptoms of a head injury, including a headache, dizziness, confusion, disorientation, difficulty thinking and memory problems. She underwent a CT-Scan and testing and was diagnosed with a concussion without loss of consciousness, a mild form of traumatic brain injury. After our client completed physical and occupational therapy, we submitted a demand package with detailed information regarding traumatic brain injury (TBI), and the case was settled for policy limits.

## Policy Limits for Client with Cervical Discectomy and Fusion Surgery

Our client's vehicle was struck by a truck exiting a gas station, when she was stopped at an intersection at Blue Ridge Boulevard and Holmes Road in Kansas City, Missouri. Our client did not seek immediate medical treatment but noticed cervical pain and strain in the days following the accident. She went to her primary care physician who referred her to a neurosurgeon. She then underwent a MRI, which noted a herniated disc protruding 7mm at C3-C4 and flattening of the spinal cord at C3-4, C4-5, and C5-6 of her spine. It also confirmed multi-level cervical spinal canal stenosis with severe stenosis at C3-4, C4-5, and C5-6. Based on the exam and the imaging findings, our client's neurosurgeon recommended she undergo ACDF (anterior cervical discectomy and fusion) surgery from C3 to C6. The insurance company of the liable party paid policy limits within days after our demand package was submitted. Our firm then pursued and obtained a full recovery of the client's under-insurance policy.

### Policy Limits for Client with Bulging Lumbar Discs

Our client was traveling westbound on Interstate 670 (I-670) just east of the Broadway Boulevard overpass in Kansas City, Missouri. Traffic slowed to an abrupt stop apparently due to congestion near the Broadway Boulevard exit ramp. Directly behind our client, another driver was traveling at a high rate of speed and failed to stop his vehicle in time. He collided his vehicle into the rear of the vehicle of our client, which totaled our client's car. Our client did not feel much pain until two days after the collision, which was the first time he sought medical care. He underwent CT scans but no fractures were noted. Our client was recommended to physical therapy, which he was unable to complete due to worsening pain. An MRI was ordered which revealed multiple bulging lumbar discs in his spine along with central canal stenosis with thecal sac effacement. Our client was recommended for injections and further physical therapy. The case settled for policy limits of the at-fault driver after our firm prepared and submitted a demand package.

**Double Recovery Against Deceased Drunk Driver**

Our clients, a married couple, were stopped in their vehicle at a red light at the intersection of State Line Road and Red Bridge Road / College Avenue. While they were waiting for the light to turn green, their vehicle was struck violently from behind by another driver. Our clients both went to the emergency room for treatment and were diagnosed with neck and back strain / pain (Cervicalgia). Their injuries from the accident did not subside for months and required physical therapy and follow up medical care. After an investigation, we found the at-fault driver was issued a DUI at the scene and that he had been involved in another, second collision nearby. Unfortunately, our investigation also determined that this driver died after the crash from an unrelated cause. We preserved our client's claim by initiating suit and requesting the court to appoint a defendant ad litem to act on behalf of the deceased defendant. Ultimately, the insurance company agreed to settle the claims for both our clients in an amount far in excess of their past and future medical bills and lost wages.

**$527,000 Judgment for Dog Bite Victim**

Our client was attacked by two vicious dogs when she was visiting her father's apartment residence in Wyandotte County, Kansas. The dogs were owned by the property owner who resided nearby and were known to have attacked other visitors and had allegedly killed another dog. Our client sustained severe bite injuries to her legs, hips and buttocks, which required surgery. Unfortunately, these injuries became infected, which required hospitalization and further treatment. We initiated suit, and after a hearing, the judgment was entered against the landowner in the amount of $527,000, which was roughly five times the amount of our client's medical bills.

**$125,000.00 Trip & Fall Settlement Helps Client with Rare "Brittle Bone" Condition**

Our client was a college student who suffered from a rare genetic disorder known as osteogenesis imperfecta ("OI"). OI is a disease characterized by the weakening of bones and is sometimes referred to as "brittle bone disease." This condition limited our client's mobility to a powered wheel-chair, which he controls. Our client was visiting an art museum with friends and was attempting to exit the building. As he moved his wheelchair through the doorway, his wheelchair hit an unmarked step that caused his wheelchair to topple over and for his body to be thrown to the ground. Our client broke several bones, including his hip and right humerus (upper arm) bone. Due to the complex nature of his disease and injuries, two revision surgeries were required of previously implanted hardware in his humerus bone. Our firm engaged an expert to investigate and opine as to the ADA and safety standards of the museum exit. After submission of a demand package, a six-figure settlement was reached. The settlement more than covered our client's past and future medical bills and will assist him in continuing his education. Our client plans to attend medical school and hopes to someday become a doctor specializing in helping patients who suffer from OI.

**Day Care Shut Down After Child's Death (Confidential Settlement)**

We initiated a wrongful death suit against a day care center care in Wyandotte County, Kansas, on behalf of a mother of young child who was found dead in a crib at the center. Our investigation found that the day care center had received multiple citations from the Kansas Department of Health and Environment (KSDHE), including citations for failure to follow safe sleep practices. After we filed suit, the KSDHE revoked the day care's license, and the center permanently closed its doors. The case was settled for a confidential amount shortly thereafter.

# WHAT OTHERS ARE SAYING

Below are some testimonials from those we have worked with in the past. As you will discover, the issues you encounter do not have to be difficult, and help is available.

*"Kevin was very professional, but approachable and friendly. He kept me informed of the progress of my case and fought for me to receive the maximum I could receive. He finished my case in a few months, after I had been waiting for two years under another attorney."*

-Kathleen, Johnson County, Kansas

*"Kevin McManus works hard for his clients and cares about his community. He represented me on a car accident case. Without his help, I would have been left with unpaid bills for my injuries and would never have received the compensation I deserved."*

-Steve, Kansas City, Missouri

*"Kevin McManus is an excellent lawyer and a wonderful person. He cares about his clients and works very hard to obtain the very best results. I have worked with Kevin on several cases and have been very impressed with his work. Kevin is an absolute pleasure to work with, and he treats everyone like family."*

-Scott Shachtman, Co-counsel

*"Kevin is a great lawyer who is very responsive. He is well known in the community and can handle many different types of practice areas. I fully recommend him as an attorney."*

-Phyllis Norman, Referring Attorney

# FREE BOOK FOR ACCIDENT VICTIMS IN MISSOURI AND KANSAS

Great news! A free book is now available for victims of car or other injury accidents in Missouri and Kansas. There is no obligation or cost with requesting this book, and you should request it today before you talk to an insurance adjuster or hire an attorney.

Copy and fill out this form and mail or e-mail this form back to us to learn:

- Who will pay my medical bills?
- Will I be paid for the time I'm losing from work?
- Should I give a recorded statement to the insurance adjuster or sign his or her forms?
- What do I do if the person who hit my car doesn't have car insurance?
- What if I don't make a full recovery and cannot return to work?

- How will I know if the insurance company's settlement offer is fair?
- Should I hire an attorney to represent me, and if so, how do I find the right one?

To receive this free book, just photocopy this form, fill it out and e-mail or mail it to us.

Email to: AccidentBook@KevinMcManusLaw.com or mail to Kevin McManus, 1100 Main Street, Suite 2600, Kansas City, MO 64105.

Please send me a free copy of: *Crash Course: An Insider's Guide to Accident & Injury Law in Missouri & Kansas,* by Kevin J. McManus

Name:

______________________________________________

Address:

______________________________________________

City:___________________________ State:

___________ Zip: _______________

**We do not share mail lists with anyone!**

# FREE INFORMATIONAL NEWSLETTERS

Want to know:

- How to best deal with insurance company denials?
- How to protect yourself from financial ruin?
- Legal insider tips about Kansas and Missouri law?
- How current legal issues and cases may affect you?
- Specific steps you can take to find the best lawyer for your case?
- Practical advice about buying insurance from one who does not sell insurance?

These are some of the topics that are covered monthly in our **free newsletter** that is available to you.

Our firm strongly believes that most legal disputes could be avoided if people had a better general knowledge about the legal system, insurance coverage, and the insurance claim process.

There is absolutely no cost or obligation to receive our newsletter, and from time to time, we run contests to give away free items!

Don't worry, this is not the boring, "canned" newsletter that most firms buy and add on their name. We write it ourselves to encourage people to pay more attention to their legal affairs.

If you later feel like you want to stop receiving our newsletter, there is a phone number in every issue that you can call to "unsubscribe."

To receive this newsletter, just photocopy this form, fill it out and e-mail or mail it to us. Email to: Newsletter@KevinMcManusLaw.com or mail to Kevin McManus, 1100 Main Street, Suite 2600, Kansas City, MO 64105.

Please send me your free legal newsletter:

Name:

__________________________________________

Address:

__________________________________________

City:__________ State: __________ Zip: ____________

If you would also like to receive our **email** newsletter, please include your email here:

E-mail:__________________________________

**We do not share mail/email lists with anyone!**

Made in the USA
Monee, IL
04 November 2026

67381851R10038